A HANDS-ON GUIDE TO

School Program
EVALUATION

by
Edward A. Brainard

Published by
Phi Delta Kappa Educational Foundation

Cover design by Victoria Voelker

Library of Congress Catalog Card Number 96-70381
ISBN 0-87367-493-6
Copyright ©1996 by Edward A. Brainard
Phi Delta Kappa Educational Foundation
Bloomington, Indiana U.S.A.

ACKNOWLEDGMENTS

Several able educators in the field of program evaluation gave generously of their time and insight to review this handbook and provide thoughtful suggestions. They include Evelyn Harding, Coordinator of Program Evaluation, Aurora (Colorado) Public Schools, and Rodney Killian, Executive Director of Student Assessment, Jefferson County (Colorado) Public Schools. Additionally, some able principals, district administrators, and education consultants reviewed a draft of this publication and provided helpful ideas. They include Sue Clark, Dan Colvin, Eugene Howard, Kathryn Kirkpatrick, Stanley Pursley, Ann Simone, Dudley Solomon, Kenneth Vedra, and David Wood.

TABLE OF CONTENTS

INTRODUCTION

This book is a result of many years of experience as a teacher, principal, director of research and evaluation, professor, philanthropic foundation executive, and assistant superintendent of schools. In all of these roles, at least some of my time was devoted to conducting program evaluations, in addition to reviewing evaluation projects done by colleagues and others. At the same time, in each position I faced other demanding responsibilities that presumably took priority. By finding ways to streamline the evaluation process without reducing its quality or effectiveness, I was able to carry out both my "regular" work and program evaluation without "burning out." Sharing that straightforward, streamlined strategy is the intent of this book.

Recently Dan Colvin, principal of South Middle School in Aurora, Colorado, described the problem facing many practicing educators who need — or are required — to conduct program evaluations. Colvin said: "The school's staff and I are engaged each day in the teaching and learning processes and in all other aspects of operating our school. At the same time, we know we have a responsibility to periodically evaluate, on a systematic basis, our various programs for students. This is certainly true for educators with a commitment to school improvement and renewal."

Colvin noted that "quick and convenient 'how to do it' program evaluation materials that guide staff members and committees save time and assist in preventing 'false starts.' Evaluating programs is important for the renewal of each endeavor we organize for the education of our students."

Mike Johnson, superintendent of School District 70 in Pueblo, Colorado, similarly comments: "A problem many school districts face is that they don't have a process in place to plan and evaluate their programs. These processes are not in place because school personnel and communities see it as too time-consuming. Evaluation is one part of a total program. Practical program evaluation processes that we can use in our district and schools are important for the health of each program we provide for our students."

The purpose of this book is to address these problems — to provide a hands-on, simple, succinct, "how to" guide to program evaluation. Using a step-by-step approach to the evaluation process, I guide the educator through the process from beginning to end in a way that is both easy to follow and easy to implement. But if the educator follows the steps outlined in this publication, then the evaluation also will be thorough and successful.

This book is designed for educators at all levels, whether their focus is the classroom, the school, the district, the state department of education, or another agency devoted to education. While the examples provided in this handbook are drawn totally from schools and districts, educators serving in state education departments and other education-oriented agencies will find many useful ideas and suggestions. This hands-on guide is not designed for highly formal studies, such as a dissertation. Instead, the program evaluation processes I describe are geared to action research principles that will be implemented directly by busy educators. This approach to evaluation uses effective low-cost practices that educators can employ *while* they continue in their primary responsibilities as teachers or administrators.

Certainly, whenever a program is developed and implemented, one fundamental question must be asked: How will we know if this program works? Over the years I have talked with hundreds of school people. Many seem puzzled about how to conduct an effective program evaluation. The process, unfortunately, often is viewed as too complicated and too time-consuming. Thus many programs are implemented, expanded, reduced, or eliminated on the basis of conjectures, assumptions, or ill-founded conclusions, instead of on sound, systematic evaluation. A sound evaluation will provide answers better than will gut impressions and guess work.

Most program evaluation is not focused on eliminating a program. Rather, the intent of the vast majority of program evaluations is toward building on strengths — renewing programs and improving programs. And, in cases where a program evaluation functions as a needs assessment, the thrust may be toward adding a new program or enlarging an existing one.

The information in this handbook is divided into three major sections. Chapter 1 examines the reasons for evaluating education programs and addresses the role that program evaluation plays in improving education practices and learning opportunities for students. This chapter also presents a list of qualities for a program evaluation and contrasts education research and program evaluation.

Chapter 2 discusses how to develop, conduct, and conclude a program evaluation. I describe the 10 sequential steps of a sound evaluation process. The reader will find a number of worksheet and checklist ideas that can be "customized" by evaluators for various circumstances. The purpose of these devices is to assist in both making and recording decisions throughout the 10 steps.

Finally, in Chapter 3, I shift gears to provide "how to do it" resources and suggestions. For example, one section describes how to develop effective surveys and includes actual survey items illustrating various criteria. Another section provides directions for conducting focus group interviews and gives examples of discussion questions. Other sections provide information and suggestions on other aspects of the program evaluation process, as well as ideas for using various quantitative data measures and qualitative information sources.

This handbook should serve as a valuable tool to assist in the important work of evaluating school and district programs. It provides a simple, comprehensive process that tells busy educators what they need to know about program evaluation: *what to do* and *how to do it.*

CHAPTER 1

The Purposes of Program Evaluation

Effective program evaluation is a systematic process that focuses on program improvement and renewal and on discovering peaks of program excellence. Program evaluation should be viewed as an important ongoing activity, one that goes beyond research or simple fact-finding to inform decisions about the future shape of the program under study.

In many cases comprehensive information about a program is so lacking that school officials not directly involved in the program can neither accurately describe a program's activities nor comment convincingly on its results, much less make informed decisions about the program's future. Therefore, program evaluation is, first of all, a way of providing information to those involved both directly and indirectly in a given program.

Second, and more important, evaluation should help those who direct and implement a program to do their jobs well. Program evaluations are strongest when they are tailored specifically to the program as it is operating in the particular school or district. This means that evaluation should proceed from a base of specific information and, often, specific questions. As Michael J. Austin and his colleagues put it: "Evaluation is useful in either confirming our suspicions or hunches or filling in some gap in our knowledge of how a program is working. In either case, we are talking about reducing uncertainty, not providing the final word" (Austin et al. 1982, p. 10).

The words, "reducing uncertainty, not providing the final word," bear repeating. Program evaluations provide information and insight but typically not the entire picture. The "final word" generally is developed after an evaluation project is completed. Later on, I will describe this final process, in which the evaluators and other decision makers "evaluate the evaluation" and address such questions as, What do the results mean to us? and What are the next steps?

Program Evaluation and Education Research

To be clear about the purposes of program evaluation, it may be useful to contrast evaluation with education research. Typically, education research is "basic research," while program evaluation may be characterized as a form of "applied research." This contrast is defined by L.R. Gay, who says that applied research is:

> more concerned with "what" works best than with "why." Basic research is concerned with establishing general principles of learning; applied research is concerned with their utility in educational settings. (Gay 1992, p. 9)

Charles F. Kettering (1876-1958), the famous inventor who for many years was the chief of research for General Motors Corporation, described the dynamic nature of research in the applied-research sense. His practical description mirrors the ideals of program evaluation. Kettering said:

> Research is a high-hat word that scares a lot of people. It needn't. It is rather simple. Essentially, research is nothing but a state of mind — a friendly, welcoming attitude toward change . . . going out to look for change instead of waiting for it to come. Research for practical [people] is an effort to do things better and not be caught asleep at the switch. . . . It is the problem-solving mind as contrasted with the let-well-enough-alone mind. . . . It is the "tomorrow" mind instead of the "yesterday" mind. (*CFK, Ltd.* 1970, p. 1)

Another label for the type of applied research that characterizes program evaluation is *action research*. Action research is not a new idea; it has been on the education scene for about 50 years as a process used by educators who desire to better understand and improve their professional practices and the educational programs provided for students.

Some years ago Walter R. Borg described some of the key differences between formal education research ("basic research" in this context) and action research, which I have relabeled as "program evaluation" in the contrasts that follow. Borg's contrasts concern project goals, measurement, data analysis, application of results, and required training (Borg 1963, pp. 319-22).

Goals

Education Research: "To obtain knowledge that will be generalizable to a broad population and to develop and test educational theories."

Program Evaluation: "To obtain knowledge that can be applied directly to the local . . . situation."

Measurement

Education Research: "An effort is made to obtain the most valid measures available. A thorough evaluation of available measures and a trial of these measures usually precedes their use in the research."

Program Evaluation: "Less rigorous evaluation of measures than in scientific research."

Data Analysis

Education Research: "Complex analysis often called for. Inasmuch as generalizability of results is a goal, statistical significance is usually emphasized."

Program Evaluation: "Simple analysis procedures usually are sufficient. Practical significance rather than statistical significance is emphasized. Subjective opinion of participating teachers is often weighted heavily."

Application of Results

Education Research: "Results are generalizable, but many useful findings are not applied in educational practice. Differences in training and experience between research workers and teachers generate a serious communication problem."

Program Evaluation: "Findings are applied immediately . . . and often lead to permanent improvement."

Required Training

Education Research: "Extensive training in measurement, statistics, and research methods is needed."

Program Evaluation: "Only a limited training in statistics and research methods is needed because rigorous design and analysis are not usually necessary."

Five Characteristics of Effective Program Evaluation

A number of experts speak of *utility*, *feasibility*, *propriety*, and *accuracy* as characteristics of effective program evaluation (Joint Committee on Standards for Educational Evaluation 1981, pp. 13-14; and 1994, pp. 5-6). To these four characteristics, I add *relevance*.

Utility concerns the need for the program evaluation to be timely and influential and to serve the practical information needs of the school or school district.

Feasibility recognizes that each program evaluation consumes valuable school district resources and, therefore, must be undertaken within the context of available resources in terms of staff time, expertise, and funding, both to manage the evaluation and subsequently to use the results.

Propriety recognizes that a program evaluation project needs to be conducted ethically.

Accuracy means that a program evaluation needs to produce sound, precise data and objective information.

Relevance means that the focus of a program evaluation and the information-gathering methods need to meet the objectives of the evaluation. Relevancy also is determined by the extent to which a program evaluation provides results that are helpful in developing or improving the program.

CHAPTER 2

The Program Evaluation Process

Leadership is the key to an effective evaluation. Therefore, accepting the leadership role or selecting an individual to provide leadership to the evaluation is a preliminary decision that must be made.

At the school level, examples of educators who typically provide leadership for a program evaluation project are a principal, an assistant principal, an administrative assistant, a department chairperson, or a staff member from a particular level or department. At the district level, leadership may be provided by a superintendent or an assistant superintendent, a director or supervisor of a particular area or function, or another staff member with broad responsibilities.

The evaluation leader must have a clear sense of the scope and thrust of the evaluation and must be capable of working with diverse constituencies, of communicating effectively, and of facilitating group discussion and decision making.

Once this leadership role has been established, then the following 10 steps should be taken to conduct the evaluation. Later, I will describe each step in greater detail.

The 10-Step Evaluation Process

Organization and Design Phase

Step 1. Develop a steering committee to guide the evaluation.
Step 2. Select the focus for the program evaluation.

Step 3. Select the information sources that will be needed for the program evaluation.

Step 4. Establish a timeline or schedule for the evaluation.

Step 5. Develop or select the instruments or forms for collecting information — quantitative, qualitative, or both.

Information Collection and Analysis Phase

Step 6. Collect information.

Step 7. Analyze the information and summarize the results.

Conclusion Phase

Step 8. Prepare the initial written report.

Step 9. Share the results with the stakeholders in the evaluation.

Step 10. Develop a follow-up action plan.

While following these 10 steps cannot guarantee a high-quality evaluation, it should lead to an evaluation that is thorough, thoughtful, and credible. Must every evaluation follow all 10 steps? Probably not. If the evaluation goal is limited or the focus is narrow, then the evaluation might take some shortcuts. On the other hand, all 10 steps probably will be essential for a large-scale or comprehensive evaluation. Indeed, some steps may need to be expanded or elaborated to meet broader or more intricate goals.

Most evaluation projects take weeks or months to complete. Therefore, a systematic approach, such as the 10-step process described here, is one way to set down a road map for the evaluation. Otherwise, individual evaluators or teams of evaluators can be deflected from the central focus of the evaluation by side issues. A clearly defined, sequential process also combats the ebbing of enthusiasm that naturally occurs whenever an evaluation process stretches over a long time. Accomplishing each step provides a moment of closure, a moment when evaluators can celebrate their accomplishments before moving on to the next step. Thus the 10-step process can help to sustain enthusiasm over the course of a major evaluation.

Important Terms

Four specific terms are used throughout this guide:

Quantitative data are numerical. Old-style researchers refer to this type of information as "hard data." These data include such measures as student counts, activity counts, percentage of participation or success, and so on.

Qualitative information is descriptive. What students or teachers do, how activities are structured, and so on, are interpreted and described, typically in narrative form.

Formative evaluation refers to program evaluation that is aimed at renewal or reform. Herman, Morris, and Fitz-Gibbon speak of formative evaluation as a "focus on providing information to planners and implementers on how to improve and refine a developing or ongoing program" (1987, p. 26).

Summative evaluation, on the other hand, seeks "to assess the overall quality and impact of mature programs for purposes of accountability and policymaking" (Herman, Morris, and Fitz-Gibbon 1987, p. 26).

Organization and Design: Steps 1 Through 5

One evaluation project began this way. The principal, two teachers who chaired different staff committees, and the learning coordinator met to discuss their school's progress toward meeting the goals of a national school restructuring program that the school had joined. Many staff development and other activities had already taken place. And, of course, over the months of involvement, each of these individuals had received various sorts of feedback from several members of the staff. However, as they discussed the schoolwide effort, they decided that they needed a more comprehensive understanding of the staff's views and how individual staff members saw the program, its strengths and weaknesses, and how the school's effort might be stimulated and improved.

This meeting led naturally to some basic questions: What do we need to know from the staff about our school's progress in achieving the goals of the national program? What has been the effect of the staff development work? How can we improve what we have been doing?

This sort of beginning is typical of how an evaluation project begins. In this case, it was not just a single school leader who stepped up but rather a team of leaders, under the authority of the school principal, who initiated the process. This group — either as it came together or expanded to include other staff in leadership positions — fulfills the intent of Step 1.

Step 1. Develop a steering committee to guide the evaluation.

In the program evaluation process, the suggested initial step is to organize a small group of colleagues — a steering committee — to establish specifications for the program evaluation project.

The job of this steering committee of colleagues includes: 1) discussing the key questions to be answered by the evaluation, its focus and scope; 2) organizing the effort, deciding who is to do what; 3) conducting or directing information-gathering activities; and 4) analyzing the information so that it can be summarized and so that conclusions can be drawn and recommendations can be developed by those involved with the program being evaluated.

The steering committee should include individuals who can bring needed expertise to the evaluation project. Keeping the group small helps not only to make discussions and decision making manageable but also to increase "ownership" in the process. Therefore, developing such a steering committee should not be a difficult or time-consuming task. And the small group size facilitates open discussion, making it easier to reach agreement on evaluative processes that are practical and well-suited to the clear purpose of the evaluation.

In some cases of large-scale program evaluation, it is necessary to develop a large committee in order to provide representation from a broad constituency. In this type of situation, it may be possible to structure a small leadership group drawn from the larger group to act as the actual steering committee for the evaluation.

The main initial work of the steering committee is to define the purposes for evaluation and to state, in concrete terms, the objectives for the evaluation project. One way to begin this work is to discuss this *key question*: What do we desire to know about the program to be evaluated?

Following are some suggested questions that may be used to expand this initial discussion:

- What are the characteristics and distinctive features of the program to be evaluated?
- How will the results of the evaluation be used?
- Are there questions that other people not on the steering committee might have about the evaluation?
- What data and information are currently available about the program?
- What resources will be needed to conduct the evaluation project?
- What are the time limits? When are the results needed?
- What decisions might be based on the evaluation? Who should be involved in making decisions?

And, either initially or eventually, the steering committee also must consider this question: Is there really a need for the proposed program evaluation project? Presuming that the answer to this question is "yes," the work of the steering committee on this step should be summarized and set down in writing. These are the two questions that will set the stage for the entire evaluation project:

> *What do we want to know about the program as a result of this evaluation?*
> *What is the purpose of this evaluation project?*

The answers to these questions should be achieved by common agreement among the members of the steering committee and shared with those who will be affected by the evaluation — in other words, the stakeholders in the evaluation.

Step 2. Select the focus for the program evaluation.

The second step in the program evaluation process is to select the best focus, which is a means of bringing clarity to the intent and purposes of the evaluation.

After isolating the purpose(s) of a program evaluation in Step 1, the selection of a focus will assist in further narrowing the scope of the evaluation. Additionally, it will help identify the group or groups from which data and information will be needed.

The checklist that follows will serve as a basis for discussion because it provides 11 different possible points of focus. By using this checklist, the steering committee can refine and target the purpose identified for the evaluation. Each of the items is discussed following the checklist.

Choosing an Appropriate Evaluation Focus

Rate each item on the checklist according to the following scale:

> 3 - an appropriate focus
> 2 - a somewhat appropriate focus
> 1 - not an appropriate focus
> 0 - not sure/don't know

1. Do we want to obtain the *views of the staff involved with the program*?
2. Do we want to obtain a *comparison of the actual program results with the expected results*?
3. Do we want to *review currently available student achievement data or obtain additional data*?
4. Do we want to *evaluate the current instructional materials or proposed new materials for the program*?
5. Do we want to obtain the *views of those affected by the program*?
6. Do we want to *assess student effort toward learning*?
7. Do we want to obtain a *comparison of the actual program with its design*?
8. Do we want to conduct an evaluation of the program in relation to the program's original goals?
9. Do we want to obtain a *review of the program by colleagues*?
10. Do we want to obtain a *review of the program by authorities*?
11. Do we want to obtain a *comparison of the program with similar programs in other schools or districts*?

A rating system is suggested. A useful starting point is to ask each steering committee member to rate the items, and then the group can proceed to discussion after eliminating clearly inappropriate items and gaining a preliminary sense of priorities. For most evaluations, one focus should be chosen in order to obtain maximum clarity in the evaluation; however, practically speaking, many evaluations attend at least to some extent to two or three focal points.

Following are descriptions of the possible focus points from the preceding checklist:

Views of the staff involved with the program. Basic questions for this type of evaluation will seek staff assessment of what is strong about the program and what might be improved. For example, if the program being evaluated is an aspect of the curriculum, evaluators might seek information about the strengths and shortcomings of such things as the textbooks, the media center print and non-print materials, the budget, technology and software, supplementary learning materials, curriculum guides, instructional equipment, and the physical facilities. This focus is often used as a first phase of the curriculum revision process.

Comparison of actual program results with the expected results. This focus often is valuable in evaluating an academic or learning area, such as mathematics or language arts. However, its value also extends to most other endeavors of a school or district, such as shared decision making or examining the school's climate for learning. Most areas of school and district operations have a set of goals, objectives, and organized activities to achieve the objectives. In this focus, expected success is checked against actual results.

Review currently available student achievement data or obtain additional data. This focus is not entirely different from the previous one. But in this case, student achievement data are the primary interest. Such data may include test scores, the distribution of academic grades, performance assessment, and alternative assessments.

Evaluate the current instructional materials or proposed new materials for the program. This focus isolates materials in order to stress their worth to the program. "Materials" can be construed to include both equipment and consumables: textbooks, media center print and non-print materials, technology and software, supplementary learning materials, curriculum guides, and instructional equipment.

Obtain the views of those affected by the program. This focus seeks information from the "customers" of the program being evaluated. Those affected by a school or district program may include students, parents, other staff members, and representatives from business, industry, postsecondary education institutions, and other levels of schools within the district.

Assess student effort toward learning. This focus looks at student commitment to out-of-class and in-class learning activities. This crucial component of student success is difficult to assess but can provide important information about an instructional program.

Compare the actual program with its design. This focus often is used a year or two after a curriculum revision. The basic question of this focus concerns the extent to which the program is operating as envisioned. Another example: When a district begins a shared decision-making program, the planners usually have in mind the shape of the new program and may develop the concept in writing. This type of evaluation will compare that written design to what really happens in various schools or offices when decisions need to be made.

Conduct an evaluation of the program in relation to the program's original goals. In this approach the results of a program are judged in relation to the original needs identified for the program, rather than against the achievement of specific objectives. For example, if the overall intent of a school in developing shared decision making is to increase stakeholder involvement, then information on the extent of involvement by students, staff, and others would be obtained; and the evaluation also might look for further objective data on the effectiveness of the program.

Obtain a review of the program by colleagues. This focus uses the process of a schoolwide evaluation to assess the merits of a single program. Over the years the North Central Association of Colleges and Schools, other regional accrediting agencies, and state departments of education have developed school evaluation programs. Such programs are designed to evaluate the school as an entire unit; that is, every program of the school is evaluated during the same time frame. Schools can adapt that evaluation concept to focus on a single program.

In this adaptation those involved with the program being evaluated conduct an analysis (in NCA terms, a "school or institutional self-study") of the program. They also provide recommendations for themselves. A small visiting team of colleagues from inside or outside the school district reviews the analysis and provides a summary of program strengths and recommendations for improvement. The final phase is the development of an action plan based on the recommendations from the self-study and the visiting resource team. (See Chapter 3 for more information about this design.)

Obtain a review of the program by authorities. This focus is identical to the previous one except that members of the visiting review team are authorities in the field, rather than colleagues from within the school or from other schools. These authorities may come from higher education or from business and industry, depending on the nature of the evaluation. (Like the previous focus, this type of design is dealt with in greater detail in Chapter 3.)

Compare the program with similar programs in other schools or districts. In this focus the program being evaluated is analyzed in relation to one or more similar programs operating in other schools within the district or in another district. If a district-level program is being evaluated, then similar programs in other districts are reviewed. Examples of factors that might be analyzed are the curriculum, instructional materials, physical facilities, and budget. Evaluation techniques may include such activities as site visits, serving on North Central Association or similar types of visiting teams, using rating scales to guide visits, and discussions with colleagues associated with the institutions selected for comparison.

When one of the preceding points of focus has been chosen, that focus, along with any secondary points of focus, should be summarized in written form. This will be a foundation document for the evaluation.

The next several steps of evaluation deal with defining and designing assessment measures, developing schedules, and gathering information.

Step 3. Select the information sources that will be needed for the program evaluation.

After selecting the focus for the program evaluation project, the next step usually involves: 1) determining the types of information needed to achieve the purposes of the evaluation, 2) selecting the best quantitative measures or qualitative information sources that will support the evaluation, and 3) identifying the populations from whom to seek input.

The basic discussion question at Step 3 is: What measures or information sources should we employ for the evaluation? Both quantitative and qualitative information should be considered; neither form excludes use of the other, though one or the other may be more appropriate for a given focus.

Note: In order to complete this step, readers may wish to skip ahead to Chapter 3. Techniques for gathering both quantitative and qualitative information are discussed there in some detail. For readers more familiar with various measures and information sources, the following checklist may be self-explanatory.

The checklist on page 19 can be used to summarize the evaluation steering committee's decisions about information sources.

Part of making decisions about what sources of information to use for evaluation also concerns the target population from whom information will be sought. For example, the warehouse supervisor in a large school district desired to gain the views of the warehouse's "customers," employees of the district, regarding warehouse services. As is the case with many district warehouses, this one provided crucial logistical support for the entire district's operations at all levels, from bus transportation to classroom supplies. The warehouse personnel were responsible both for delivering supplies ordered directly by the schools from vendors and for warehousing large quantities of expendable supplies (papers, pencils, etc.), which the schools then ordered from the warehouse. Most of the direct

Choosing Information Sources

The following sources will be used for evaluation. Check all that are appropriate.

Quantitative Measures

_____ survey

_____ discrepancy evaluation model

_____ rating scale

_____ checklist

_____ modification of the Delphi technique

_____ tests

_____ standardized tests

_____ performance assessments

_____ other quantitative data. Specify.

Qualitative Information

_____ structured interview

_____ focus group interview

_____ nominal group process

_____ school self-studies and visiting team reports

_____ adaptation of the North Central Association process

_____ observations

_____ documents, records, and materials

"customers" were secretaries in various school and central administration offices, as these employees usually were responsible for making certain that needed supplies were on hand when needed. As a result, a questionnaire was sent to this population, and interviews were conducted with a small sample of secretaries.

Thus the last part of Step 3 is to identify the population(s) from which evaluative information is needed. For each quantitative measure and qualitative information source checked in Chart 2, the steering committee should identify a matching target population. For example, if "rating scale" is checked, who will complete the rating scale?

A Word About Sampling. When the target population for gathering information is quite large, the steering committee may wish to consider sampling, rather than attempting to gather information from every member of the population. Krijcie and Morgan (1970) provide a chart of appropriate sample sizes. For example, if the target population for a staff survey is 50 persons, the sample size should be 44. Obviously, in this case it would be more convenient and logical to send the survey to the entire staff and forget about the idea of sampling. However, if the target population is 200 persons, then sampling the recommended number of 136 may be considerably easier.

Sampling can be a rather complex procedure, but the potential for using sampling should not be overlooked. However, the steering committee also should be prepared to respond to "public relations" concerns. While sampling often saves time and resources, it can leave evaluation leaders open to questions from staff members who were not sampled and who may complain, "Why didn't they ask me? Why wasn't I included?"

Step 4. Establish a timeline or schedule for the evaluation.

At this point the steering committee should list the 10 steps of the evaluation and place a target completion date next to each step. However, it should be kept in mind that some dates may need to be changed because of unforeseen circumstances and that some steps may need to be revisited. While the steps are ordered logically, not every evaluation will proceed in a strictly sequential manner.

Step 5. Develop or select the instruments or forms for collecting information — quantitative, qualitative, or both.

Step 5 connects directly to Step 3. In Step 3, decisions were made regarding the information sources to be tapped for the evaluation project. Step 5 establishes how to gather the information. Because this is such a crucial step, I will deal extensively with the development and selection of information-gathering tools in Chapter 3. Suffice it to say at this point that the array of potential instruments includes tests, surveys, questionnaires, and opinion polls, many types of which are available from educational and commercial publishers. However, in many cases a "homemade" instrument may better fit the exact purposes and locale of the study. Therefore, in Chapter 3, I also will address some of the key issues in developing effective information-gathering tools.

Information Collection and Analysis: Steps 6 and 7

Step 6. Collect information.

Once the information-gathering methods and instruments have been developed or selected, Step 6 is the process of collection. For example, a questionnaire must be distributed in some fashion and then collected. Small-scale or informal surveys may be simply handed out to participants and then collected at a later time. Or the surveys may be completed during a general meeting. For example, if a questionnaire is designed to gather opinions about a specific school program, the questionnaire might be handed out at a faculty meeting. The group might be given time to complete the questionnaire during the meeting and the survey collected at the close of the meeting.

For a larger or more formal survey, it may be necessary to mail the questionnaire to potential respondents, providing a postage-paid envelope for the return of the completed survey. And, of course, the same is true for other types of information-gathering instruments.

Likewise, face-to-face information gathering through personal interviews or focus groups must be scheduled and carried out in a manner that produces systematic results.

Step 7. Analyze the information and summarize results.

In Step 7, program evaluators must begin the important work of pulling together the information they have gathered. Most information will be either qualitative or quantitative. Therefore, it makes good sense at this juncture to say a few words about how these two types of information might best be summarized.

For summarizing *qualitative* information:

- Report verbatim responses for small surveys. If the number of respondents and the number of questions are both small, it may be possible simply to report survey respondents' comments verbatim.

- Consider reporting results by topic or by question. For example, to report on structured interviews, summarize the responses to each question using broad categories and indicate the number of responses in each category. If questionnaire responses are contradictory, report the various viewpoints.

Here is how one evaluation team reported the responses they received from teachers who were asked: "What are the advantages of having students remain with the same teaching team for their three years of middle school education?"

Observations of the teachers:

The program provides students with three years of school stability and continuity.

Having the same teacher for a three-year period provides students with one type of stability in their lives.

Students receive a three-year program not only in academics, but also in behavior growth. Negative student behaviors are not repeated year after year.

At the beginning of each school year, a minimum of academic time needs to be devoted to review and "start up" activities. And, at the end of the school year, less time has to be devoted to concluding activities.

Over the summer break, students receive homework assignments and activities, expanding the learning time period.

For summarizing *quantitative* data:

- Consider using a measure of central tendency. These measures include calculations of a *mean* (arithmetic average of responses), *median* (midpoint between response extremes), or *mode* (most-often selected response). Of these, the *mean* is used extensively as an indicator; and it is relatively easy to calculate.
- Consider using the *standard deviation* as a measure of variability. It indicates how narrowly or broadly results are spread out in relation to the mean. For example, in a normal

distribution, plus or minus one standard deviation should include about two-thirds (68%) of the responses. Plus or minus two standard deviations should include about 95% of the responses.

- Consider using *percentages* to indicate proportionate results from simple response scales or *frequencies* to record numbers or percentages of respondents making the same response. When the number of respondents is about 20 or more, *percentages* typically are more useful in describing results.
- When appropriate, provide a test of significance. Two commonly used statistics are the "t-test, which is used to see if there is a significant difference between the means of two groups" (Gay 1992, p. 291), and the "analysis of variance, which is used to see if there is a significant difference among the means of three or more groups" (Gay 1992, p. 291).

Standard statistics reference books can provide information about these common statistical tools. Following is an example of how one evaluation team summarized the responses to a survey question.

Survey Question: How comfortable are you in stating your opinions about the school district's programs, even if you disagree with the approach being taken?

Results and Response Scale:

Response	Administrators
N=83	
1: Uncomfortable	7%
2: Somewhat uncomfortable	14%
3: Somewhat comfortable	34%
4: Comfortable	45%

Mean = 3.2
Standard deviation = .91

Summary: About 8 out of 10 of the district's administrators reported that they were either "somewhat comfortable" or "comfortable" in stating their opinions even if they disagreed with the approach being pursued.

Another way to summarize the responses to this survey question is to use a simple bar graph to visually display the results. That graph might look like this one:

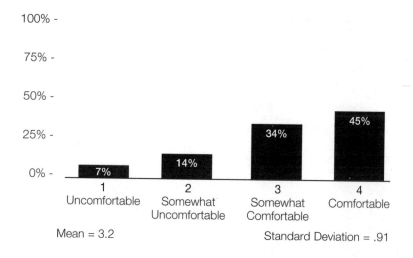

My point in these examples is to demonstrate that results summaries should be as direct and stated as simply as possible. If the results are tallied by a computer, the statistics program will provide the mean, standard deviation, percentages, and tests of significance, should such be appropriate. However, a common calculator can be used to compute means and percentages. If the standard deviation is desired, use a scientific calculator.

Conclusion: Steps 8, 9, and 10

Step 8. Prepare the initial written report.
Step 7 rolls into the conclusion phase as part of the final report. The written report should be as condensed as possible. One major purpose of the report is to stimulate discussions among those who can and will make use of the results. Such people do not have unlimited time to examine every nuance of the results. Highlighting key results is a valuable service for busy educators. In addition to — or in lieu of — a written report, in some instances the report can be presented in a visual form. Longer

reports, when length is necessary, will benefit from the inclusion of a report summary, or "executive summary."

Following are the elements of an effective report:

- Purpose of the program evaluation.
- Background information, if appropriate.
- Time frame in which the program evaluation was conducted.
- Who conducted the program evaluation. (Include the names of the small steering committee who assisted with planning and conducting the evaluation.)
- Specific topics covered by the program evaluation.
- Brief description of the population or populations who provided evaluative information.
- How the results were analyzed.
- Summary of results, in most cases reported by topic.

Note that this list does not include conclusions and recommendations. If the potential users of the report wrestle with the results through group discussion, then the value of the program evaluation will be enhanced and the results made more meaningful. After all, those who are responsible for delivering the program that was evaluated must be the ones to improve the program. They are the ones, in the final analysis, who must draw conclusions from the evaluation and then develop recommendations and action plans. That is the intent of Step 9.

Step 9. Share the results with stakeholders in the evaluation.

Obviously, the main audience for the results of a program evaluation are those most likely to use the results. Such an audience might be a staff team, department, or other unit within a school or from several schools throughout a district. Some of these individuals almost certainly served on the evaluation project steering committee. At this stage, that group needs to be enlarged so that the evaluation results can be discussed.

There also may be several secondary audiences, such as the staff of the entire school or district or some other group, such as a curriculum committee or a parent group.

One way to involve stakeholders in using the results of a program evaluation is to develop a workshop. Depending on the size of the group, individuals, teams of two, or subgroups might each take a section of the written report and assess that section, drawing conclusions that they then share with the others. Out of this sharing should come the development of action steps to be taken for program improvement. Thus this forum can be useful in creating the action plan that is Step 10.

Step 10. Develop a follow-up action plan.

A large number of reference books on planning provide information on action planning. The actual plan, of course, will depend on the type of project evaluated and what needs to be done to improve it. I include this step merely to emphasize the importance of making use of the results of the evaluation.

An effective action plan should answer the following questions:

- What will the plan accomplish (the objectives)?
- What activities are needed to achieve the objectives?
- Who will be responsible for carrying out the activities?
- What is the target completion date for each activity?
- What will serve as evidence of success for each activity?

These 10 steps create a complete evaluation cycle. Once the action plan is carried out, another evaluation cycle may be useful to assess whether the planned improvements were achieved. Evaluation seldom is fully useful as a "one-shot" solution. Rather, evaluation is more usefully viewed as ongoing and cyclic.

CHAPTER 3

Resources for Conducting Evaluation Projects

The purpose of this chapter is to provide "how to" information concerning the quantitative data measures and qualitative information sources previously discussed. Specifically, this chapter presents principles, concepts, and suggestions concerning the development and use of the following types of information-gathering tools:

Quantitative Data Measures
Surveys (questionnaires, opinion polls)
Discrepancy evaluation model
Rating scales
Checklists
Modification of the Delphi technique

Qualitative Information Sources
Structured interviews
Focus groups
Nominal group process
Adaptation of the North Central Association (NCA) school evaluation process

These two sections are interdependent. The discussion of principles, concepts, and suggestions for developing surveys, for example, is relevant to the development of rating scales, focus groups, and so on. Therefore I have attempted to avoid the redundancy of repeating obvious similarities among the instruments after I have initially stated the common principles.

A word about pilot testing is in order. To ensure that surveys and other information-gathering instruments can do the job for which they are intended, it often is useful to pilot test "home-made" instruments. For example, if a student survey is being developed, evaluators might ask a small group to complete the survey and to identify any items they do not understand. Later, such items can be rewritten. Several drafts may be necessary in order to fine tune the instrument.

Evaluation leaders might want to consider holding a steering committee meeting before actually writing any items so that the group can discuss what needs to be covered along with what the actual items for each topic might look like. While a worksheet is not essential for this activity, it is a good idea to list in one column each needed instrument and in another column the person responsible for developing or locating that instrument.

Quantitative Data Measures

Surveys. As one means of obtaining quantitative data, surveys are valuable and popular. Surveys come in various forms, such as questionnaires or opinion polls. Many of the examples in this section and the sections that follow are drawn from actual instruments used in schools and districts. Most of the examples are adapted from instruments that I have developed for various purposes.

Because of their usefulness and adaptability, I have included a full-scale survey as Appendix A. That example has been adapted from an actual survey used in the Aurora Public Schools in Colorado.

Following are suggestions for developing survey items, or questions. These suggestions also apply to developing items for rating scales, checklists, and questions for interviews and focus groups. (Many of these ideas are drawn from Barber, Forbes, and Fortune, *Developing Research Skills for Professional Educators*, 1988, pp. 28-29.)

1. Develop questions that are direct, concise, and easily read. Examples:

- As you see it, to what extent are decisions made in this school district based on adequate information?
- The Anytown School District is a good place to work.
- How clear would you say you are concerning the efforts of the school district for improving the K-12 science program for students?
- How important is it for the school district to use surveys of employees as one means of determining whether improvements are needed in various school district programs?

2. Choose words for survey items that the audience for the survey will understand. Example:

- How satisfied would you say you are with the efforts of the school district's administration to provide information about standards-based education?

The response scale for this question would range from "very dissatisfied" to "very satisfied." While this question would be appropriate for the district's professional staff, it might not be appropriate to ask of parents unless the term "standards-based education" is described in lay terms.

3. Develop questions that deal with only one concept at a time. For example, use:

- To what extent do you receive recognition for your accomplishments in the Anytown School District?

Do not say:

- Generally, our faculty understands and acts on processes for school renewal.

In the second example, the respondent might view the faculty as understanding the processes, but not acting on them — or vice versa. But the respondent will have no way to register this response. It is, in essence, two items.

4. Ask only questions that are needed for the program evaluation. Eliminate the "nice to know" items, keeping only the "need to know"

questions. "Need to know" survey items are those that fit closely the purposes and focus of the evaluation. Other items can creep into the survey because they would be "nice to know." But they will needlessly lengthen the instrument and diminish its effectiveness.

5. Develop clear instructions for completing the survey. For an example, see the complete survey sample in the Appendix.

6. Ask the questions in a logical sequence.

7. Pay attention to the appearance of the survey. The form should be easy to read and pleasing to the eye. Placing a space between items, for example, will help to minimize the problem of respondents accidentally skipping an item. A clear, simple, attractive format also will increase the rate of response. Again, for a complete example, see the sample survey in the Appendix.

8. Use only one or two "open-ended" survey items that require a written response. Most, if not all, survey items should be "closed-end." These are items where the respondents select one response from a response scale. Following are two examples of open-ended survey items.

- *Broad Open-Ended Survey Item:* Please list any issues that, in your view, the school district should be addressing that are not now being addressed.
- *Limited Open-Ended Survey Item:* As you see it, what are the two most important strengths of the Accelerated Schools program?

One problem in using surveys is getting enough people to return them to make the results useful. Following are several suggestions for increasing survey returns (also drawn from Barber, Forbes, and Fortune 1988, p. 28). Respondents are moved to respond to a survey when:

1. They respect the sponsor of the survey. (Suggestion: At the outset of a survey instrument, print a message from the superintendent, the principal, or the responsible staff com-

mittee, stating the purpose and importance of the survey. See the sample survey in the Appendix.)

2. They believe their response will make a valuable contribution to an important issue or program.
3. They believe the survey has been sent to them personally.
4. They can remember the information requested without having to look something up.
5. They believe their responses will be treated professionally and their privacy will be protected.
6. They believe the survey is unbiased, meaning that the survey has not been structured to yield only answers that support the biases of the persons conducting the survey.
7. They believe they will receive information about the results of the survey.
8. They can complete the survey in a short time.

This last point is particularly important. A survey instrument should be as short as possible. Short surveys avoid respondent fatigue, which can lead to the respondent quitting the survey before completion. In addition, someone has to either tally the results or prepare them for tally by computer; and then the results have to be analyzed, summarized, and organized into a report. Thus a short survey also helps the evaluation team get results more quickly.

If a survey will include more than 20 items, consider breaking it into two or more sections and sending the sections separately, perhaps a month apart, to the respondent population.

For the most part, the preceding principles have been the "do's" of surveying. Following are some of the "don'ts":

1. Avoid asking questions that request information or knowledge that respondents may not have. Example: "Most students at Ajax High School demonstrate responsibility." If such an item is posed for parents, most will not possess sufficient general knowledge of the student population to answer.
2. Avoid asking for information that is available from another source. It wastes time and energy of respondents to request information that already exists elsewhere.

31

3. Avoid using survey items that establish impractical conditions or use vocabulary that is too broad. Example: "Our principal interacts with all groups and individuals." Not only does this item contain two "questions" (groups and individuals), it also includes the conditional word, "all," which adds an unreasonable quality modifier.
4. Avoid asking respondents for their suggestions or opinions if there is reason to believe that there is little or no intent to use or consider their views.
5. Avoid asking respondents to do clerical work, such as researching records, in order to form their response.
6. Avoid asking respondents to use complex coding scales in responding to survey items. (Sample response scales are listed later in this chapter.)
7. Avoid asking respondents to rank order a list of more than six items. Instead, consider using the modification of the Delphi technique that is explained later in this chapter.
8. Avoid asking respondents for their names or other identifying information.
9. Avoid requesting private information, such as income level. Generally, such information is neither needed nor appropriate.

Examples of Different Types of Survey Items. The following examples are drawn from a variety of surveys. Each example illustrates a different type of response scale.

Survey question with a follow-up item:

- In the past year or so, what would you say have been your sources of information about the move toward year-round education in the school district? Please check as many sources as appropriate.

    ____ 1. Conversations with colleagues.
    ____ 2. General staff meetings at my school or work site.
    ____ 3. Meetings with school district administrators.
    ____ 4. Department, team, and/or grade-level meetings.
    ____ 5. The district's staff newsletter.

_____ 6. Special district publications and memos about year-round education.

_____ 7. Service on the year-round education task force.

_____ 8. Professional literature about year-round education.

_____ 9. District staff development workshops on year-round education.

- Using the above list of possible sources of information, please circle the items you feel have been your three best sources of information about year-round education.

Survey question that requests a decision:

- In an era of declining school district financial resources, would you favor any of the following modifications of school district warehouse services? Please use this response scale:

> 4 - yes
> 3 - probably yes
> 2 - probably no
> 1 - no
> 0 - don't know/not sure

_____ Delivery of common school supplies from the warehouse on a weekly rather than on a daily basis.

_____ Reduction of daily district mail service to, say, twice a week. Such a reduction means many time-dated messages would have to be sent by fax.

_____ Elimination of the moving of equipment and furniture by district employees through establishing a bid process with commercial moving firms.

Survey item that provides future marketing information:

- How did you hear about summer school? Please check as many items as appropriate.

_____ 1. From the summer school catalog delivered by U.S. mail to my home.

_____ 2. From the summer school flyer I received at school.

_____ 3. From my parents.

_____ 4. From my teacher(s) at school.

_____ 5. From my counselor(s) at school.

_____ 6. From my school's principal or assistant principal(s).

_____ 7. From my friends.

Survey item that provides an explanation before asking a question:

- Three years ago, the school district organized efforts to improve K-12 curriculum articulation between the middle schools and the high schools. In your professional judgment, to what extent has curriculum articulation improved between the middle schools and the high schools?

  _____ (4) considerable improvement

  _____ (3) some improvement

  _____ (2) articulation is about the same as in the past.

  _____ (1) articulation is worse than in the past.

  _____ (0) don't know/not sure

Following is the same type of item used in one of the annual PDK/Gallup Polls of the Public's Attitudes Toward the Public Schools:

> Some public schools in the nation have increased the amount of time students spend in school by extending the school year or school day. Do you favor or oppose increasing the amount of time students spend in the public schools in your community? (Elam 1995, p. 27)

Survey items of a general nature:

- How do you rate the extent of the success Ajax Elementary School has experienced in the transition from a traditional school year calendar to a year-round school calendar?

  _____ (5) excellent success

  _____ (4) good success

  _____ (3) average success

____ (2) fair success

____ (1) poor success

- How satisfied would you say you are with the school district's effort to provide inservice education about standards-based education?

  ____ (5) very satisfied

  ____ (4) satisfied

  ____ (3) neither satisfied nor dissatisfied

  ____ (2) dissatisfied

  ____ (1) very dissatisfied

- In your professional judgment, how effective are the currently available instructional materials for supporting the curriculum in (name of area)? Please use this rating scale.

  5 - excellent

  4 - good

  3 - average

  2 - fair

  1 - poor

____ textbooks

____ supplementary learning materials

____ technology

____ media center print materials

____ audiovisual materials

____ instructional equipment

- The school district provides a professional atmosphere for staff.

  ____ (5) agree

  ____ (4) somewhat agree

  ____ (3) neither agree nor disagree

  ____ (2) somewhat disagree

  ____ (1) disagree

- How do you rate the quality of education received at the most recent school your child or children attended in the Anytown Public Schools?

  ___ (5) excellent
  ___ (4) good
  ___ (3) average
  ___ (2) fair
  ___ (1) poor

A semantic differential scale "asks an individual to give a quantitative rating to the subject of the attitude scale on a number of bipolar adjectives such as good-bad, friendly-unfriendly, positive-negative. . . . In practice, however, these dimensions are frequently ignored and/or replaced by other dimensions thought to be more appropriate in a particular situation" (Gay 1992, p. 173). The format of the traditional semantic differential scale for a student survey follows:

- What is your assessment of this course? Place an X on one of the five lines between each pair of words.

boring	__ __ __ __ __	interesting
confusing	__ __ __ __ __	clear
uninformative	__ __ __ __ __	informative

The major problem with this type of scale is that respondents select choices both on the horizontal lines and between the lines, which makes tallying the results difficult. The survey item at the top of page 37 avoids this problem by using a modified format. Some of the terms for this example were drawn from Orlich (1989, pp. 372-73).

Sample Response Scales for Surveys. Many types of response scales can be used with "closed-end" or "forced-choice" survey items. Often in developing surveys, educators do not have readily available a resource list of the wide range of possible response

A survey item with a modified format.

DIRECTIONS (when used as a pre-survey): Please place an X in the box between the paired phrases to indicate your desires for this course.

DIRECTIONS (when used as a post-survey): Please place an X in the box between the paired phrases to indicate your opinion on how this course was actually delivered.

	Low ＊	Somewhat Low ←	Balanced ↔	Somewhat High →	High ＊	
1-Conducted by lecture as primary format						1-Conducted with hands-on experience
2-Course goals clearly specified and followed						2-Course goals outlined but flexible depending on student needs
3-Information oriented						3-Practice oriented
4-Passive participation (reading, writing, etc.)						4-Active participation (discussion, problem solving, group work, etc.)
5-Independent learning						5-Instructor stimulated learning activities
6-Oriented toward problems in general						6-Oriented toward specific problems
7-Primarily information giving						7-Balanced among lectures, activities, demonstrations

scales. As a result, they sometimes limit their thinking to a few commonly used response choices, such as:

> strongly agree
> agree
> neither agree nor disagree
> disagree
> strongly disagree
>
> yes
> no
>
> almost always
> frequently
> occasionally
> seldom
> almost never

However, it is not necessary to use the same response scale for all of the items or questions of a survey. In fact, depending on the purposes of the survey, it often is desirable to use more than one type of response scale. In developing a survey, an interesting technique is to try selecting the response scale or scales first. While this may seem backwards, surprisingly this strategy actually helps in writing the items or questions. It is especially helpful in selecting the verbs for the items, thereby ensuring parallel construction of the items.

Following is a list of 35 different response scales. Some of these scales include four responses without the opportunity to select a neutral or "fence-sitting" position. Others include the neutral response, such as "neither agree nor disagree." Whether one limits choices to positive and negative responses will depend on the specific situation and the purpose of the survey. However, in such cases it sometimes is appropriate to add the "don't know/not sure" category. For example, a recent survey of parents asked: "How satisfied are you with the provisions our school makes for academically outstanding students?" The response scale was: "very satisfied, satisfied, dissatisfied, very dissatisfied"; and the "don't know/not sure" category was added to the end of the scale, because many parents would not be familiar with the opportunities provided to such students. The resource list that follows can stimulate ideas for tailoring a survey to specific circumstances.

very limited extent
some extent
considerable extent
great extent

little understanding
some understanding
much understanding
great deal of understanding

poor quality
fair quality
average quality
good quality
excellent quality

definitely very helpful
helpful
neither helpful nor not helpful
not helpful
definitely not very helpful

strongly disagree
disagree
neither disagree nor agree
agree
strongly agree

disagree
somewhat disagree
neither disagree nor agree
somewhat agree
agree

definitely no
no
neither yes nor no
yes
definitely yes

no
generally no
neither yes nor no
generally yes
yes

limited to no value
some value
average value
considerable value
great value

declined
somewhat declined
about the same
somewhat improved
improved

too hard
about the right amount
not hard enough

not important
somewhat not important
not sure/don't know
somewhat important
important

definitely will not
probably will not
don't know/not sure
probably will
definitely will

very dissatisfied
dissatisfied
neither satisfied nor dissatisfied
satisfied
very satisfied

dissatisfied
somewhat dissatisfied
neither satisfied nor
    dissatisfied
somewhat satisfied
satisfied

inappropriate
somewhat inappropriate
neither appropriate nor
    inappropriate
somewhat appropriate
appropriate

oppose
somewhat oppose
neither oppose nor support
somewhat support
support

poor
fair
average
good
excellent

almost never
seldom
about 50% of the time
usually
almost always

much more
more
about the same
less
much less

almost never
seldom
occasionally
frequently
almost always

little or no emphasis
less emphasis
about the same emphasis
more emphasis
much more emphasis

very ineffective
ineffective
neither effective nor ineffective
effective
very effective

ineffective
somewhat ineffective
neither effective nor ineffective
somewhat effective
effective

very inappropriate
inappropriate
neither appropriate nor
  inappropriate
appropriate
very appropriate

definitely not important
not important
neither important nor unimportant
important
definitely important

undesirable
somewhat undesirable
neither desirable nor undesirable
somewhat desirable
desirable

greatly discourage
discourage
neither discourage nor encourage
encourage
greatly encourage

insufficient
somewhat insufficient
neither insufficient nor
  sufficient
somewhat sufficient
sufficient

not at all beneficial
not beneficial
somewhat beneficial
beneficial
very beneficial

poor preparation
below average preparation
average preparation
above average preparation
well prepared

disfavor
tend to disfavor
neither favor nor disfavor
tend to favor
favor

unsatisfactory
somewhat unsatisfactory
neither satisfactory nor
  unsatisfactory
somewhat satisfactory
satisfactory

strongly disagree
moderately disagree
slightly disagree
slightly agree
moderately agree
strongly agree

very insufficient
insufficient
neither insufficient nor
  sufficient
sufficient
very sufficient

Format Suggestions for Survey Instruments. Typically, surveys are printed on one or more sheets of standard 8½" x 11" paper or 8½" x 14" legal-size paper. As a result, they often appear to be long and uninteresting. Both of these factors can reduce the rate of return. To counter this impression, consider printing the survey in the form of a small booklet. For example, one sheet of folded 8½" x 11" paper makes a four-page booklet with 5½" x 8½" pages. And one sheet of folded 8½" x 14" legal-size paper becomes a four-page booklet with 7" x 8½" pages.

One school district used the four-page format to survey members of its administrative staff. The first page of the booklet — made by folding a single, legal-size sheet — contained an introductory letter:

Dear Colleague:

Two years ago we used the Enlightened Leadership Process to gain your views on how to make the administrative staff meetings highly productive and valuable.

How are we doing? That question is the purpose of this survey, along with this question: What further improvements are needed?

At the May administrative staff meeting, you will receive the results of this survey. In addition, together we will discuss the results and next steps.

Thank you for your commitment to the education of our students.

Sincerely,

Thank You for Your Assistance
Please return by May 4

The second page of the booklet was blank, and the third page contained a short survey:

In regard to the administrative staff meetings during the current school year, *to what extent* have each of the following been achieved? *Please use this rating scale:*

4-Great Extent
3-Considerable Extent
2-Some Extent
1-Very Limited Extent

Administrative Staff Meetings

__ 1. Deal with meaningful issues/topics that are important to the district's mission.

__ 2. Have an open atmosphere for gaining administrator input.

__ 3. Are well-planned.

__ 4. Use input to affect some outcome.

__ 5. Allow time for significant interaction among administrators.

__ 6. Rarely have insignificant topics on the agenda.

__ 7. Enhance collegiality among administrators.

__ 8. Provide an atmosphere of involvement as opposed to "being talked at."

__ 9. Provide updating information concerning important issues/topics.

__ 10. Deal with the "big picture" of education.

In planning administrative staff meetings for the forthcoming school year, what should we do more of, better, or differently? *Your suggestions on this topic are encouraged.*

The fourth page of the booklet was left blank to provide ample room for people to respond to the last, narrative item in the survey.

Discrepancy Evaluation Model. The discrepancy evaluation model "involves making decisions based on a determination of the differences, or discrepancies, which exist between standards and actual performance. In other words, evaluation involves a comparison of the way things are with how they should be" (Gay 1980, p. 14).

Surveys using this model ask respondents to respond to an item or question using two responses: For one response, participants indicate the present condition, or "What Is"; and for the second response they indicate the ideal, or "What Should Be." In human endeavors, differences or discrepancies between "what is" and the "what should be" might be expected. Whether the size of any difference between the means for an item is excessive, as well as the meaning of the difference, is best determined through discussion by an assigned group.

The statistical t-test is used to determine whether the difference between the two means for an item is "significant" (meaning indicative of something other than chance).

Following is an example of a survey format using the discrepancy evaluation model adapted from Howard, Howell, and Brainard (1987, pp. 55-69). In this example, two means would be calculated and compared, one for the "What Is" column and another for the "What Should Be" column.

School Climate Survey

The purpose of this survey is to give you an opportunity to express your views about several aspects of your school's climate.

For each item, please indicate a rating in *both* the "What Is" column and the "What Should Be" column. *Please use this rating scale:*

1-Almost Never
2-Occasionally
3-Frequently
4-Almost Always

	What Is	What Should Be
1. Teachers trust students to use good judgment.	_____	_____
2. In our school low-achieving students are respected.	_____	_____
3. The goals of this school are used to provide direction for the programs offered students.	_____	_____
4. Typically, most teachers at our school use a range of teaching materials.	_____	_____
5. At our school most students get positive feedback.	_____	_____

In the above example, two means for each item would be calculated, one for the "What Is" and one for the "What Should Be" responses. The difference between the two means is determined by subtraction.

Rating Scales. This section provides two examples of rating scales. The first is a scale for rating yearly action plans developed by schools. This example is a portion of a larger rating scale, as is the second example. The second is a rating scale for evaluating performance assessments, which was developed by Evelyn Harding and others in the Aurora (Colorado) Public Schools in 1995.

Action Plan Rating Scale

Name of School_____

Directions: For each characteristic, please indicate your rating using this scale.

4-Sufficient
3-Somewhat Sufficient
2-Somewhat Insufficient
1-Insufficient
0-Incomplete Information to Rate Plan

__ 1. The plan generally represents a guide to action.

__ 2. The plan is ambitious enough to be challenging.

__ 3. The plan is cognizant of external constraints.

— 4. The plan communicates what is to be accomplished. That is, the typical person will understand what it is that is under way.

— 5. The plan is significant. That is, as a result of the effort, it will make a difference at the school.

— 6. The plan uses action verbs.

— 7. The plan indicates it is based on the needs of the school.

— 8. The plan indicates the persons responsible for achieving each objective.

— 9. The plan specifies the nature of the results. That is, the school will know when success has been achieved for each objective.

— 10. The plan indicates the target completion date for each objective.

Performance Assessment Rating Scale

Directions: Please rate the performance assessment using the following scale or rubric. The standard for such assessment follows:

The performance assessment —

- Is reflective of what is taught.
- Is readable for most students.
- Requires use of complex thinking processes.
- Is bias-free in terms of gender and ethnicity.
- Response format provides appropriate means of demonstrating knowledge of the content assessed.
- Design facilitates students' interpretation of, and response to, items.

Circle below the score you give the performance assessment.

4 — Meets all criteria of the standard and exceeds some.
3 — Meets all criteria of the standard.
2 — Meets some, but not all, criteria of the standard.
1 — Meets very few criteria of the standard.

Checklists. Following are two examples of checklists. The first represents a portion of a larger checklist that was designed for use by persons who are knowledgeable about school district public relations programs (Bagin, Ferguson, and Marx 1985, pp. 114-15). The second example, developed by the National Committee for Citizens in Education (Henderson, Marburger, and Ooms 1986, pp. 85-86), comes from a checklist for parents and deals with the same subject.

Public Relations Department Checklist

Please rate the school district's public relations program on each of the following criteria. Check (✓) the criteria that are presently an aspect of the district's program.

— 1. The Board of Education has adopted a public relations policy.

— 2. The Board of Education's policy demonstrates a commitment to public relations.

— 3. The public relations department develops a yearly action plan.

— 4. The public relations function is staffed adequately.

— 5. The public relations function has an adequate budget.

— 6. The public relations director is one of the first to know of major happenings in the district.

— 7. A two-way internal public relations plan is in place.

— 8. The public relations program has developed a plan to meet the communication needs of identified target audiences.

— 9. The external public relations program employs a variety of communication techniques.

— 10. The department has developed a crisis communications plan.

— 11. The public relations department analyzes feedback from internal publics.

— 12. The public relations department analyzes feedback from external publics.

COMMENTS:

Family-School Relationships Checklist

Please respond "Yes" or "No" for each item of this checklist.

— 1. Do office personnel greet parents (in person or on the phone) in a friendly, courteous way?

— 2. Are there directions for parents and visitors to find their way around the school?

— 3. Is there a comfortable reception area for parents and visitors?

— 4. Is there an orientation program for incoming students and their families?

— 5. Are there regular social occasions where parents and school staff can get to know each other?

— 6. Does the school permit parents to observe classes?

— 7. Does the school have an "Open Door" policy, where parents are welcome at any time during the school day?

Modification of the Delphi Technique. According to L.R. Gay, the Delphi technique "typically involves mailing questionnaires to participants, providing them with feedback on actual responses, and giving them opportunities to revise their responses. This process is repeated until consensus is reached. Of course the process results in consensus only, not necessarily in the best decisions. It is also a costly, time-consuming procedure. While at one time it was the 'in' technique, the novelty seems to have worn off and it is currently used much less frequently than it once was" (Gay 1980, p. 67).

The modification that follows avoids some of the problems inherent in the full-scale version of the technique. This modification uses a simplified one-step design, instead of the multi-step approach of the original process. The technique is a tool for determining the degree of importance of each factor in a set of factors. In addition, it is an alternative to asking respondents to rank order a number of items. In sets of six or more items, rank ordering is especially difficult.

In the following example, assume that 20 factors are to be rated. These factors would be listed in Column 1.

Modified Delphi Technique
Which Are Most Important?

Column 1	Column 2	Column 3	Column 4
List 20 items	Of the 20 items in Column 1, check the 15 most important.	Of the 15 items in Column 2, check the 10 most important.	Of the 10 items in Column 3, check the 4 most important.

Notice the "winnowing" effect. Column 2 asks for a selection of 75% of the items in Column 1. Column 3 winnows out a third of the remaining items. Finally, Column 4 reduces the 20 items considered in Column 1 to the 4 most important items.

If the procedure begins with 15 or fewer items in Column 1, it is probably wise to have only two more steps, rather than the three steps illustrated here.

With this modification of the Delphi technique, evaluators can obtain weighted numerical data. For example, each item listed in Column 1 that is checked in Column 2 would be given 1 point. If that item is carried into Column 3, it would be given another 2 points. And if the item also is checked in Column 4, it would receive an additional 3 points. The weighted data are calculated simply by adding up the total points for each item.

Qualitative Information Sources

Structured Interviews. The structured interview as a source of qualitative information is more flexible than the survey. Barbara

Perry-Sheldon and Violet Allain (1987) comment: "It is particularly useful when exploring broad dimensions of an issue that has not been clearly defined. Interviews can be informal chats or they can be highly structured with a specific sequence of questions to be asked" (p. 21).

L.R. Gay describes the interview as:

> essentially the oral, in-person, administration of a questionnaire to each member of a sample. The interview has a number of unique advantages and disadvantages. When well conducted it can produce in-depth data not possible with a questionnaire; on the other hand, it is expensive and time-consuming, and generally involves smaller samples. The interview is most appropriate for asking questions which cannot effectively be structured into a multiple-choice format. . . . In contrast to the questionnaire, the interview is flexible. . . . The interview may . . . result in more accurate and honest responses. . . . Another advantage of the interview is that the interviewer can follow up on incomplete or unclear responses by asking additional probing questions. Reasons for particular responses can also be determined.
>
> Direct interviewer-interviewee contact also has its disadvantages. The responses given by a subject may be biased and affected by her or his reaction to the interviewer, either positive or negative. (1992, p. 231)

In face-to-face interviews, as well as in focus group interviews, respondents provide "perceptions, attitudes, and a sense of why participants think and feel the way they do" (Kirkpatrick and Brainard 1994/95, p. 330).

In conducting interviews, evaluators should consider limiting the interview to a series of probably no more than three to five questions. For example, the following questions are good basics that might be used in a number of different types of evaluations.

1. What would you like to see happening in (name of program) a year from now? What about in two years? (For the program being evaluated, these are "images of potential" types of questions.)

2. If someone were moving to your metropolitan area (or city) and asked you about the strengths of (name of the program), what

would you say? What would you report concerning any needed improvements?

3. Finish this statement: If you were in charge of (name of program), you would _____. (A similar type of question is: If you had a "magic wand" and could change any aspect, what changes, if any, would you make in this program?)

4. What, if anything, should (name of program) do more of, better, or differently?

5. Please describe any issues that, in your view, (name of program) should be addressing that are not now being addressed.

With such questions in mind as a starting point, following are the basic steps to take in the interview process:

1. Determine the population to be interviewed. This should have been accomplished in Step 3 of the evaluation process, which was described in Chapter 2.
2. Develop the interview guide — the interview questions you plan to ask. Consider developing questions that require short responses. Stick to questions directly related to the program being evaluated.
3. Develop a logical sequence for the questions. It usually is best to begin with the easiest questions.
4. When requesting an interview, state the purpose of the program evaluation project and tell the interviewee how long the interview should take to complete. Generally, interviews should not consume more than 30 minutes of the person's time.
5. When beginning the interview, describe again the purpose of the program evaluation project.
6. Either at the outset of the interview or when requesting the interview, advise the respondent that his or her responses will be confidential to the extent that the information reported will not be attributed to specific, named individuals. If this is not to be the case, so advise the respondent.
7. Do the following during the interview:
   a. Take careful notes of what is said. In more formal studies, consider using a tape recorder. If a tape recorder is used,

make sure the interviewee knows the session is being recorded.

b. Be prepared to ask a follow-up question. This practice helps you to capture the complete intent of interviewee's response. Two examples of general follow-up questions are: Can you tell me more about that? In your view, for what reasons is that a strength of the program?

c. Do not hesitate to provide appropriate "feedback" during the interview by stating what you have just recorded in your notes. This gives the interviewee a chance to correct your notes. It also demonstrates that you desire to be faithful in recording the person's views.

d. Do not influence the answers. Be nonjudgmental.

e. Be considerate of the interviewee's time and avoid unrelated conversation. Keep to the interview guide's questions and to the time length that was stated when requesting the interview.

8. After the interview, summarize the results. (See Step 8 in Chapter 2 for more information about summarizing evaluation results.)

Focus Groups. In a focus group, participants are led in a discussion by a moderator. The objective is to focus the discussion on relevant topics in a non-directive manner. Focus groups are particularly effective in providing information as to why people think and feel the way they do. Such groups are used to discover opinions, attitudes, concerns, and perceptions of people about a topic, issue, program, or product.

Focus group interviews usually involve from seven to ten people and a moderator. To the extent possible, the participants should be representative of the larger target population from which evaluative information is sought. The moderator uses a set of questions as a means of stimulating and focusing the group's discussion. Bagin, Ferguson, and Marx comment:

> While some organizations use focus groups to stay in touch, others rely on these important feedback groups to

provide indications of concerns that might be tested later in more scientific surveys. In many cases, the focus group discussion begins by asking participants how they feel about an issue or program. Then the discussion moves to an exploration of how members of the group think others feel. A focus group can even assist in developing survey questions. (1985, p. 117)

In the early 1950s the focus group process was adapted from the behavioral science arena by the marketing and advertising fields as a means of examining advertising and new product concepts, such as baby food and low-suds detergents. Since then, any number of other areas have used focus group interviews.

The following focus group process is adapted from materials developed in 1995 by Doug Magee, vice president of research at MGA-Thompson Inc. in Denver, and Sue Clark, director of organizational support in the Aurora Public Schools in Colorado. Here are the basic steps:

1. Identify the purpose for conducting the focus group.
2. Identify the types of persons to be involved. The focus group usually should involve persons of a similar demographic population, such as teachers or parents. Include both "friends" and "foes." However, it usually is not wise to include employees and their supervisors in the same group, such as teachers and their principal.
3. Identify the moderator for the focus group. (The role of the moderator is outlined after this list.)
4. Develop the concept areas and questions to be covered. Generally, there are two to four concept areas, each of which may be covered by several questions in the interview session. Keep the questions simple and specific.
5. Conduct the interview. Either tape record the session or have a recorder take detailed notes. A flip chart that lists responses can be used to record the sessions, and it also allows participants to keep track of what has been said.
6. Summarize the results in writing. (See Step 8 in Chapter 2.)

The role of the moderator is important. How that individual performs can determine whether the focus group yields useful information. Following are activities that the group moderator should do:

1. Give the participants the discussion questions in advance so that they can think about the issues beforehand.

2. Supply the participants with name tags and allow the participants to introduce themselves. The tags and introductions serve as ice-breakers and help the moderator personalize comments and probe with follow-up questions. They also facilitate more personal dialogue among the participants.

3. Explain the purpose of the session and the role of the focus group. Explain what is expected of participants, how the information will be used, and how the information will be recorded. Indicate that thoughts, not names of those stating the thoughts, will be used.

4. Set a definite beginning and ending time. This helps to keep the group focused on major thoughts, rather than dealing with minutiae.

5. Encourage participation early from each participant. Keep the group focused on each topic until the participants have exhausted their pertinent comments. Encourage participants to talk to each other and not just to the moderator. As necessary, probe for more concrete statements from participants.

6. Praise individuals for their contributions. But maintain a neutral position on what is said by the participants. The moderator does not indicate any approval or disapproval of the statements made by the participants. Nor should the moderator comment on or respond to what is said by the participants, even though it may be hard to listen to negative comments or inaccurate perceptions.

7. At the end of the session, thank the group for their participation, summarize the group's main points on each topic, and indicate what will happen next with the information. This helps the group to achieve closure.

Following are examples of some questions that may be useful in thinking about the types of discussion that can be fostered in a focus group.

Questions about making decisions:
- In our district, what are our strengths in the area of decision making?
- How could we improve decision-making processes in our district?

Questions about territorial, or "turf," problems:
- It has been said there are too many turf issues among the schools and administrative units of our school district. To what extent is this your perception?
- If your response is generally "yes," what could be done to reduce or solve such problems?

Questions about how certain issues are dealt with:
- If we handle (name the issue) in this manner, what could be reactions or concerns?
- What might be a better approach to dealing with this issue?

Questions about a pilot program:
- In your professional judgment, what are the strengths of the adjusted curriculum?
- Are there areas of the curriculum that need further development?
- To what extent is the curriculum guide easy to use?
- What problems have you discovered in using the adjusted curriculum?

Nominal Group Process. The purpose of the nominal group process is to involve groups in generating solutions for problems as part of an evaluation. Stecher and Davis comment that the nominal group process:

> is a process for leading a group to identify several options
> and to select among them. It works best with small groups
> of five to nine people.

The process generally involves five steps. First, group members work individually to generate lists of options in response to a question or a problem. Second, the facilitator leads the group in a round-robin listing of options until the complete set is before the group. This is followed by a controlled discussion in which options are clarified. Questions may be asked, but attacks or advocacy regarding particular options is discouraged. Individuals then rank the options individually or express preferences in a vote. Votes or rankings are tallied and displayed. In the final step the group discusses the options again in light of the vote tally. If necessary, participants vote again until a single option or sufficiently narrow range of options emerges.

The use of controlled discussion and voting in the nominal group technique is often effective in moving groups to a speedy decision if members are willing to accept the rule. However, the discouragement of debate may prevent a full discussion of the consequences of options and does not necessarily promote the selection of the best ones. (1987, p. 90)

One school district used the nominal group process to examine four questions. The all-day session involved 56 persons representing parents and the various types of district employees: classified staff, teachers, and administrators. Using the process outlined by Stecher and Davis, each of seven subgroups considered four questions:

- How might the district further improve the instructional and curriculum systems?
- How might the district further improve the human resources management systems/processes?
- How might the district further improve communications and public relations?
- How might the district further improve its decision-making systems/processes?

Adaptation of the North Central Association (NCA) School Evaluation Process. Over the years the North Central Association of Colleges and Schools, other regional accrediting agencies, and state departments have developed school evaluation programs.

Such programs are designed to evaluate the school as an entire unit — that is, every program of the school is evaluated during the same time frame. This adaptation abbreviates this evaluation concept and focuses on the evaluation of a single program.

In this adaptation, those involved with the program being evaluated conduct an analysis (in NCA terms, a "school or institutional self-study") of the program. They also provide recommendations for themselves. A small visiting resource team of colleagues from inside or outside the school district reviews the analysis and provides a listing of program strengths and improvement recommendations. The final phase is the development of an action plan based on the recommendations from the self-study and the visiting resource team.

A prime feature of this approach to program evaluation is the high degree of involvement of the personnel concerned with the program being evaluated. This NCA-style evaluation process also provides opportunities for these persons to network with colleagues associated with similar programs in other schools and districts.

Two aspects of this type of evaluation merit further description: the self-study and the work of the visiting resource team.

The self-study by staff members of the program being evaluated can be quite brief. The chart on page 55 illustrates some sample self-study questions concerning two necessary dimensions of a typical program evaluation.

Visiting resource team members are educators or others knowledgeable about the program under study. Team members can be from the program school, from other schools in the district, or from other districts. Parents, students, personnel from higher education, or individuals from related education or social service agencies also may be asked to participate as resource team members. But it is best to keep the visiting team small, probably from two to five members in addition to the chairperson.

The chairperson is responsible for coordinating the work of the team. Evaluators should ask the chairperson to visit the program for a few hours about four to six weeks prior to the team being on

Study Questions on the Program's Present Status	Study Questions Concerning Program Improvement
What processes are now used to develop direction and improvement?	Do the processes for developing direction and improvement need to be improved? If so, what might be done?
What processes are now used to ascertain program effectiveness in relation to the program's goals and objectives?	Does program effectiveness and accountability need to be improved? If so, what might be done?
What processes are now used to establish program credibility and importance?	Does program credibility and importance need to be improved? If so, what might be done?
How does the program relate to criteria for an effective or ideal program?	Does the program need to be adjusted in relation to criteria for an effective or ideal program? If so, what might be done?

site. In addition, the chairperson should review the self-study and provide suggestions for improvement. The chairperson also should be involved in the selection of the resource team and the issuing of invitations to participate in the on-site visit.

Most visiting teams need to be on-site from one to two days. The role of the visiting resource team is to:

- Review the staff's analysis, or self-study, of the program being evaluated.
- Observe the program in action and conduct interviews, such as with staff committees, individual staff members, students, administrators, and parents.
- Prepare written and oral reports describing program strengths and suggested recommendations for program improvement.

A FINAL WORD

The focus of this guide has been to describe the program evaluation process so that busy educators can use it to examine their programs without compromising their primary responsibilities as teachers or administrators. Thus the thrust has been toward processes that are simultaneously effective, practical, and convenient.

Program evaluation projects provide educators with the information and insights they need to refine and improve the services and programs they provide to their students. And that is a worthy goal.

REFERENCES

Austin, Michael J., et al. *Evaluating Your Agency's Problems.* Beverley Hills, Calif.: Sage, 1982.

Bagin, Don; Ferguson, Donald; and Marx, Gary. *Public Relations for Administrators.* Washington, D.C.: American Association of School Administrators, 1985.

Barber, Larry W.; Forbes, Roy H.; and Fortune, Jim C. *Developing Research Skills for Professional Educators.* Bloomington, Ind.: Phi Delta Kappa, 1988.

Borg, Walter R. *Educational Research: An Introduction.* New York: David McKay, 1963.

CFK Ltd., An Education-Oriented Philanthropic Foundation. Englewood, Colo.: CFK Ltd., 1970.

Elam, Stanley. *How America Views Its Schools: The PDK/Gallup Polls, 1969-1994.* Bloomington, Ind.: Phi Delta Kappa Educational Foundation, 1995.

Gay, L.R. *Educational Evaluation and Measurement: Competencies for Analysis and Application.* Columbus, Ohio: Charles E. Merrill, 1980.

Gay, L.R. *Educational Research: Competencies for Analysis and Application.* 4th ed. New York: Merrill-Macmillan, 1992.

Henderson, Anne T.; Marburger, Carl L.; and Ooms, Theodora. *Beyond the Bake Sale: An Educator's Guide to Working with Parents.* Columbia, Md.: National Committee for Citizens in Education, 1986.

Herman, Joan L.; Morris, Lynn Lyons; and Fitz-Gibbon, Carol Taylor. *Evaluator's Handbook.* Newbury Park, Calif.: Sage, 1987.

Howard, Eugene; Howell, Bruce; and Brainard, Edward. *Handbook for Conducting School Climate Improvement Projects.* Bloomington, Ind.: Phi Delta Kappa Educational Foundation, 1987.

Joint Committee on Standards for Educational Evaluation. *Standards for Evaluations of Educational Programs, Projects, and Materials.* New York: McGraw-Hill, 1981.

Joint Committee on Standards for Educational Evaluation. *The Program Evaluation Standards: How to Assess Evaluations of Educational Programs.* 2nd ed. Thousand Oaks, Calif.: Sage, 1994.

Kirkpatrick, Kathryn, and Brainard, Edward. "Images for NCA's Future: Perceptions in One State." *NCA Quarterly* 69 (Fall 1994-Winter 1995): 330.

Krijcie, R.V., and Morgan, D.W. "Determining Sample Size for Research Activities." *Educational and Psychological Measurement* 30 (1970): 607-10.

Orlich, Donald C. "Evaluating Staff Development: Four Decision-Making Models." *The Clearing House* 62 (April 1989): 372-73.

Perry-Sheldon, Barbara, and Allain, Violet Anselmini. *Using Educational Research in the Classroom.* Fastback 260. Bloomington, Ind.: Phi Delta Kappa Educational Foundation, 1987.

Stecher, Brian M., and Davis, W. Alan. *How to Focus an Evaluation.* Beverley Hills, Calif.: Sage, 1987.

Sample Survey

This appendix provides a sample of a full-scale survey. This instrument, adapted from an actual survey used in the Aurora Public Schools in Colorado, was used to gather information from soon-to-be-graduated high school seniors about their impressions of their high school education. This survey is somewhat longer than might be considered usual. One reason for the instrument's length was purely tactical, as the seniors were to complete their survey while other students were taking a portion of an achievement test battery. Otherwise, this survey would have been divided into several instruments.

At various points in the survey, I have added explanatory notes, which are printed in brackets to avoid confusing them with the survey itself.

Cover Letter

Dear Senior:

Congratulations on your forthcoming graduation!

Each year our district conducts studies about several of its programs for students as one means of discovering ways to improve high school education.

Your completion of this survey will be of great assistance to your school.

Sincerely,

[Note: The names of the principals of the district's high schools were listed.]

Senior Survey

1. Which high school do you now attend?
[Checklist provided.]

2. For how many years did you attend high school in the Aurora Public Schools?
_____ (1) Either one year or less than one year
_____ (2) Two years
_____ (3) Three years
_____ (4) Four years

3. Did you attend middle school for one or more years in this district?
_____ (1) Yes
_____ (2) No

4. Did you attend elementary school for one or more years in this district?
_____ (1) Yes
_____ (2) No

[The above four questions were included for demographic purposes. With such information, one can analyze results by school, by years of high school attendance, and by attendance or non-attendance in the district's middle schools and elementary schools. Furthermore, with the above information and with items 28 and 29 of the survey, one also can analyze the results against any of the other items that follow.]

5. What are your primary occupational or educational plans for the coming fall? (Please check one of the following.)
_____ (1) Not sure at this time
_____ (2) Full-time employment
_____ (3) Attend a two-year college
_____ (4) Attend a four-year college or university
_____ (5) Attend a business, technical vocational, or trade school
_____ (6) Military service
_____ (7) Other (Please specify) _____

6. If you plan to continue your education in the fall, please check one of the following.

_____ (1) I plan to attend school in another state.

_____ (2) I have not yet made a final choice of which school I will attend.

_____ (3) I plan to attend a school, college, or university in this state. If so, please check below which institution you plan to attend.

[Note: At this point, the names of the state's major postsecondary institutions were listed.]

7. If you plan to continue your education beyond high school, do you plan to work while you are in school?

_____ (1) Yes, vacation periods only (summer, Christmas, spring break, etc.)

_____ (2) Yes, part-time work while attending school

_____ (3) Yes, full-time work while attending school

_____ (4) No

_____ (5) Not sure at this time

8. How much education do you expect to complete by the time you are 25? (Please check the highest level you expect to complete.)

_____ (1) High school only

_____ (2) A vocational or training course other than college

_____ (3) Some college or university work

_____ (4) Four years of college or university (a college or university degree)

_____ (5) Graduate degree from a college or university

9. To what extent have you developed your career goals?

_____ (1) My career goals are quite firm. I know what I want to do.

_____ (2) I have some idea of what it is I want to do for a career.

_____ (3) I am unsure of my career goals at this time.

_____ (4) I have not given much thought to my career goals.

10. In high school, do you feel that your were required to work too hard, work about the right amount, or not hard enough?

_____ (1) Too hard

_____ (2) About the right amount

_____ (3) Not hard enough

11. How interested in school were you while in high school?

_____ (5) Definitely very interested

_____ (4) Interested

_____ (3) Neither interested nor disinterested

_____ (4) Not interested

_____ (5) Definitely not very interested

12. Listed below are the subject fields offered by your high school. For each area listed, please respond to the questions indicated in both Part I and Part II for those areas in which you took classes.

PART I	SUBJECT AREA	PART II
Approximately how many credits did you take in each area listed while in high school? *Please use this response scale:* 1-No credits taken 2-*Less than two* credits taken 3-*Two or more* credits taken		For you, how valuable was the content or subject matter in each area in which you took classes? *Please use this response scale:* 1-Limited value 2-Some value 3-Average Value 4-Considerable Value 5-Great Value
	a. Art	
	b. Business Education	
	c. Computer Science	
	d. English (including Reading and Composition)	
	e. Foreign Language	
	f. Home Economics	
	g. Industrial Arts	
	h. Journalism	
	i. Mathematics	
	j. Music	
	k. Physical Education	
	l. Science	
	m. Social Studies	
	n. Special Education	
	o. Speech and Drama	
	p. Vocation-Technical Education	

13. Listed below are the activities offered by your high school. For each activity, please respond to questions 1 and 2.

Activities	1. Did you participate? Circle "Yes" or "No" (1) (2)	2. If you participated, how *valuable* was participation to you?				
		Limited Value (1)	Some Value (2)	Average Value (3)	Considerable Value (4)	Great Value (5)
a. Athletics	Yes No					
b. Clubs	Yes No					
c. Drama	Yes No					
d. Intramural Sports	Yes No					
e. Music	Yes No					
f. Speech & Forensics	Yes No					
g. Student Government	Yes No					

14. To what extent do you feel that school-sponsored activities outside the classroom (such as sports, clubs, pep rallies, etc.) contribute to school spirit?

_____ (5) Definitely very helpful

_____ (4) Helpful

_____ (3) Neither helpful nor not helpful

_____ (2) Not helpful

_____ (1) Definitely not very helpful

15. From which of the following sources did you receive assistance in making your educational, vocational, or career plans? (Please check as many of the following as appropriate.)

_____ (1) Teachers

_____ (2) Counselors

_____ (3) Courses (subjects) studied

_____ (4) Friends

_____ (5) Parents

_____ (6) Career fairs, career days, career weeks

_____ (7) Your own interests, experiences, research

_____ (8) Other. Please specify _____

16. In making your educational, vocational, or career plans, how valuable was the assistance you received from each of the following? (Please check as many of the following as appropriate.)

	Limited Value (1)	Some Value (2)	Average Value (3)	Considerable Value (4)	Great Value (5)
a. Teachers					
b. Counselors					
c. Courses (subjects) studied					
d. Friends					
e. Parents					
f. Career fairs, career days, career weeks					
g. Your own interest, experiences, research					

17. How do you feel about the discipline *you* experienced in high school? Was it too strict, not strict enough, or just about right?

_____ (1) Too strict

_____ (2) Just about right

_____ (3) Not strict enough

_____ (4) Not applicable. I did not experience any discipline while in high school.

18. In your opinion, do you feel that discipline *in general* in your high school needs to be more strict, less strict, or remain about the same as now?

_____ (1) More strict

_____ (2) Remain about the same as now

_____ (3) Less strict

_____ (4) Don't know/not sure

19. Please indicate your degree of satisfaction with each of the following aspects of your high school.

	Very Dissatisfied (1)	Dissatisfied (2)	OK (3)	Satisfied (4)	Very Satisfied (5)
a. Condition of the building					
b. Condition of the classrooms					
c. Media Center materials					
d. Media Center facility					
e. Student attitude toward learning					
f. Quality of instruction					

19. *(Continued)* Please indicate your degree of satisfaction with each of the following aspects of your high school.

	Very Dissatisfied (1)	Dissatisfied (2)	OK (3)	Satisfied (4)	Very Satisfied (5)
g. School's interest in students					
h. School's guidance and counseling program					
i. School spirit					
j. Learning atmosphere					
k. Students' kindness to one another					
l. Social activities					
m. Science laboratory facilities					
n. Other instructional laboratories (such as Industrial Arts, Business Education, Art, etc.)					
o. Programs in career education and planning					
p. Provisions for students needing special assistance in improving skills, such as in reading and mathematics					
q. Provisions for academically talented students, such as honors programs, accelerated courses					

20. Now that you are graduating from high school, you are able to judge how well you have learned certain skills and knowledge. Please rate your preparation for each item listed below.

	Poorly Prepared (1)	Below Average Preparation (2)	Average Preparation (3)	Above Average Preparation (4)	Well Prepared (5)
a. Reading skills					
b. Writing skills					
c. Mathematical computation skills					
d. Solving problems					
e. Appreciation of American heritage					
f. Making decisions					
g. Taking tests					
h. Working independently					
i. Speaking skills					
j. Appreciation of art					
k. Interpreting information from maps, graphs, charts					
l. Human relations skills					
m. Appreciation of music					
n. Library and research skills					
o. Listening skills					

20. *(Continued)* Now that you are graduating from high school, you are able to judge how well you have learned certain skills and knowledge. Please rate your preparation for each item listed below.

	Poorly Prepared (1)	Below Average Preparation (2)	Average Preparation (3)	Above Average Preparation (4)	Well Prepared (5)
p. Using sources of information					
q. Responsibilities of good citizenship					
r. Appreciation of literature					
s. Reading for enjoyment					
t. Spelling					
u. Knowledge of grammar					
v. Study skills					
w. Physical fitness and sport skills					
x. Leadership skills					
y. Taking responsibility					
z. Functioning cooperatively with others					
aa. Writing legibly					
bb. Organizing ideas in writing					
cc. Following oral instructions					
dd. Summarizing readings					
ee. Drawing reasonable conclusions					
ff. General employability skills (punctuality, attendance, work ethic, etc.)					

21. How would you rate your attitude toward learning while in high school?

_____ (5) Excellent

_____ (4) Good

_____ (3) Average

_____ (2) Fair

_____ (1) Poor

22. Did you have a job while in high school (not including summer vacation employment)?

_____ (1) Yes. If YES, please answer questions 22a through 22e.

_____ (2) No. If No, please go to question 23.

22a. Which year(s) did you work? (Please check as many years as appropriate.)

_____ (1) Freshman

_____ (2) Sophomore

_____ (3) Junior

_____ (4) Senior

22b. In your current (or most recent) job, how many hours per week do you work? (Do not include summer employment.)

_____ (1) 1-5 hours

_____ (2) 6-10 hours

_____ (3) 11-20 hours

_____ (4) 21-30 hours

_____ (5) 31-40 hours

_____ (6) More than 40 hours

22c. In your current (or most recent) job, are more than half of your hours worked on the weekend? (Do not include summer employment.)

_____ (1) Yes

_____ (2) No

22d. Is your current (or most recent) job related to your future occupational plans? (Do not include summer employment.)

_____ (1) Yes

_____ (2) No

22e. What type of work do you do in your current (or most recent) job? (Do not include summer employment.)

23. On the average, how many hours of television would you say you watch per day on weekdays during the school year?

_____ (1) 0-1 hour

_____ (2) 1-2 hours

_____ (3) 2-3 hours

_____ (4) 3-4 hours

_____ (5) More than 4 hours

24. How many books would you say you have read in the past two months simply for enjoyment?

_____ (1) None

_____ (2) One

_____ (3) Two

_____ (4) Three

_____ (5) Four or more

25. What are some of the things that helped you do well in school?

26. Is there something you wish that your high school had done to make your education more valuable?

27. Is there something you wish that you yourself had done to made your education more valuable?

[Note: Generally a survey should probably not include more than one open-ended item.]

28. Please indicate the following:

_____ (1) Female

_____ (2) Male

29. Please indicate the following:

_____ (1) American Indian/Alaskan Native

_____ (2) Asian/Pacific Islander

_____ (3) Black

_____ (4) Hispanic

_____ (5) White

_____ (6) Other

THANK YOU FOR YOUR ASSISTANCE.

Over the years, Edward Brainard has conducted program evaluation projects for numerous schools and districts. His career in education includes serving as assistant superintendent of the Aurora (Colorado) Public Schools, secondary school principal and director of research and evaluation for the Jefferson County (Colorado) Public Schools, assistant professor at Kansas State University, professor at the University of Northern Colorado and director of the Colorado state committee of the North Central Association of Colleges and Schools, director of educational grants for the Charles F. Kettering Foundation, and president of CFK (Charles F. Kettering) Ltd., an education-oriented philanthropic foundation. Following military service, he began his education career as a junior high school teacher in Billings, Montana.